The Adventures of Scuba Jack
Copyright 2021 by Beth Costanzo
All rights reserved

While many fascinating animals live in Antarctica, one of the coolest is the **gentoo penguin**. Gentoo penguins are some of the most recognizable penguins on our planet. Even though you may not travel to Antarctica to see these adorable creatures, it's worth taking the time to explore why they are so amazing.

Gentoo penguins like to eat crustaceans. For example, they love to munch on krill. They also enjoy eating squid, squat lobsters, and fish. Because of this, the gentoo penguin's diet is high in sodium. But to avoid some of the things that happen with a high sodium diet, the gentoo penguin has a salt gland that can remove sodium from its body.

Gentoo penguins are known for the wide white stripe that is on top of their heads. While baby gentoo penguins don't have it, you can see this stripe when looking at adult male or female gentoo penguins. Along with this, these penguins have an orange-red bill and a very prominent tail. These penguins are generally two to three feet tall and weigh around 15 to 20 pounds.

Like other animals in our oceans, gentoo penguins need to protect themselves from many different predators. Some of those predators can include killer whales, leopard seals, and sea lions. However, gentoo penguins also need to protect themselves from land predators. Some of these land predators are skuas and giant petrels, but they only go after baby gentoo penguins.

While there is much more to the gentoo penguin, I hope you can see how interesting it is.

It is an adorable animal that plays a large part in its ecosystem.

Gentoo Penguin

Write the correct answer in the box

What do Gentoo Penguins like to eat?

1- Leaves

2- Plants

3- Crustaoceans

Write the correct answer in the box

How much do Gentoo Penguins weigh?

1- Around 5-10 pounds

2- Around 15-20 pounds

3- Around 25-35 pounds

Write the correct answer in the box

Where do Gentoo Penguins live?

1- Africa

2- Antartica

3- Australia

Write the correct answer in the box

Do Gentoo Penguins have predators?

1- Yes

2- No, they don't.

Gentoo Penguin Activities

Trace then rewrite the phrase below.

Count the penguins then circle the answer.

8 9 10	8 9 10
10 9 11	10 9 11

Maze

Help the Penguin to find its way

Gentoo Penguin Craft

Visit us at:
www.adventuresofscubajack.com

www.ingramcontent.com/pod-product-compliance
Lightning Source LLC
Chambersburg PA
CBHW060429010526
44118CB00017B/2423